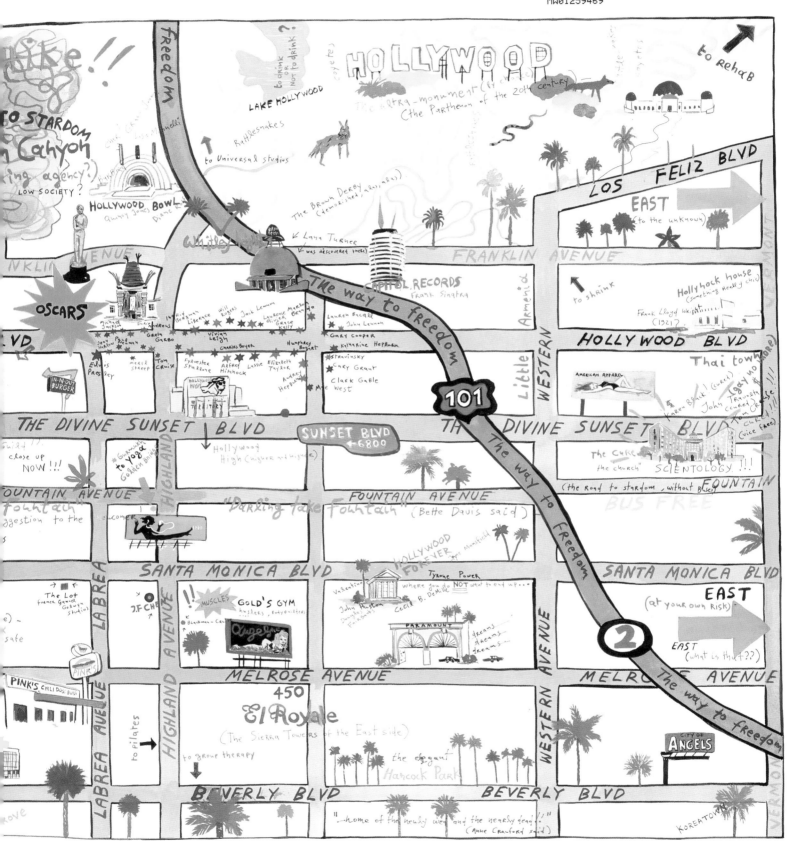

CITY OF DREAMS
LOS ANGELES INTERIORS

RIZZOLI

New York · Paris · London · Milan

CITY OF DREAMS
LOS ANGELES INTERIORS

INSPIRING HOMES OF ARCHITECTS, DESIGNERS, AND ARTISTS

ANNIE KELLY
PHOTOGRAPHY BY TIM STREET-PORTER

CONTENTS

INTRODUCTION

Los Angeles is a big city for one book. If there is a common architectural thread running through this metropolis, it is diversity—from the Hollywood origins where anything was possible to the warm year-round climate where life takes place both indoors and outdoors. Los Angeles features an incredible variety of housing, ranging from a modern art-filled cube overlooking the ocean in Malibu to an adaptive-reuse loft in a 1929 Hollywood office building, to a Venetian Gothic villa sporting a Juliet balcony, complete with a gargoyle. Art is another thread in this city's fabric, and with Los Angeles now part of the international art world, many homeowners here have built important collections, and resident artists have created work for others as well as their own spaces. Today, many designers are inspired by the rich legacy of this city's architectural and interior design evolution and have added their own twenty-first-century touches. To put their accomplishments in perspective, the following is a sweeping history of some of the most iconic, historic houses and interior decorating styles.

This is the city of dreams. Here is where the film industry moguls came and hired designers to create Spanish Colonial as well as early Modernist houses for themselves. Attracted by the year-round crisp, bright sunlight, they arrived in Los Angeles around 1910, bringing a strong view of how interiors, past and present, should look on celluloid. Hollywood attracted European émigrés, many of whom became the heads of Hollywood studios. Samuel Goldwyn, Louis B. Mayer, and Carl Laemmle came, respectively, from Poland, Russia, and Germany. By 1921 more than 80 percent of the world's cinema was produced in Los Angeles, and the creation of elaborate and evocative film sets became a serious business to entertain an increasing and enthusiastic audience.

OPPOSITE: Spanish Colonial architecture became popular in the 1920s and still defines much of Los Angeles. In the foreground is a view of the 1920 planned community of Whitley Heights showing a house once owned by Edward James, the English collector and patron of surrealist art in the 1940s.

Others flocked to Los Angeles. In the early years of the twentieth-century, East Coast residents also started to winter in Pasadena, California, bringing with them a keen interest in Arts and Crafts; in 1908, David and Mary Gamble, who had moved to California from Cincinnati, commissioned a house by architects Charles and Henry Greene. Called the Gamble House, it is one of the finest examples of the American Arts and Crafts movement, especially as it still contains all the original furniture designed by the architects.

With LA's growing population, postwar housing was especially needed. The freedom to build on undeveloped land led to some of the best mid-century domestic modernist architecture in America being built in Los Angeles. Architects from abroad were lured by the freedom to create in the mild climate and empty spaces of Los Angeles. Austrians Rudolph Schindler and Richard Neutra arrived in the 1920s; they had a profound influence on twentieth-century architecture in Los Angeles.

Frank Lloyd Wright's influential first house in Los Angeles was the Hollyhock House, built between 1919 and 1921 for the oil heiress Aline Barnsdall. Today, movies like *Blade Runner* and the television show *Westworld* can be recognized by their iconic Frank Lloyd Wright locations. Versions of his buildings created for the film *North by Northwest*, as well as TV shows such as *Game of Thrones* and *Lucifer*, continue to show his influence.

As movies were released years after the early planning stages, set designers moved ahead of current trends toward avant-garde ideas that they anticipated becoming mainstream. When Cedric Gibbons, head of MGM's art department, visited Paris's 1925 *Exposition Internationale des Arts Décoratifs et Industriels Modernes*, he brought the art deco style to Hollywood, and from there, through celluloid, to the world. His interiors were some of the most beautiful seen on film. In 1929, he decorated a sleek modernist-style house in Santa Monica for his bride, the actress Dolores del Rio.

In 1924, set designer William Cameron Menzies created the vast Moroccan-style sets for the *Thief of Baghdad*, which were a sensation. They inspired the prevailing Spanish Colonial style of building in Hollywood to sprout

OPPOSITE: **The Arts and Crafts dining room of the 1908 Gamble House, showing how Greene and Greene architects integrated the furniture with the architecture.**

extra arches and cupolas on their terra-cotta-tiled roofs. This film also had a profound influence on set decorator and designer Tony Duquette, who was still using similar pagodas and banners in his work seventy years later in the 1990s.

The years immediately before and after World War II were a glamorous period for Los Angeles. The city became a mecca for writers, architects, artists, composers, socialites, intellectuals, and even aristocrats fleeing the Nazi threat in Europe. During the 1930s, the designer of note was actor-turned-decorator William "Billy" Haines, who introduced French and English antiques and a new design style best described as Hollywood Regency.

OPPOSITE, TOP: The 1922 Schindler House is an example of early Los Angeles modernism. OPPOSITE, BOTTOM: Cedric Gibbons designed the Dolores del Rio House in 1929; it was inspired by a seminal art deco exhibition held in Paris in 1925. ABOVE: The art deco–style Cary Grant Theatre, honoring MGM studio's days, can be found on the Sony Pictures lot in Culver City.

Tony Duquette was also deeply inspired by the films of early Hollywood. After serving in World War II, he became a decorator, who was mentored by costume designer Adrian as well as the most famous "Lady Decorator"—Elsie de Wolfe, who became Lady Mendl. She had sought refuge from her beloved France in Beverly Hills during the war and took Duquette under her wing; he created furniture for her and her clients. Probably the most iconic Duquette image is his much-published drawing room at Dawnridge, which reflects both his European influences and his vision of Hollywood glamour. Here, he included his first piece of furniture commissioned by de Wolfe, who famously asked him to create a *meuble*.

Twentieth-century Los Angeles has some of the world's best representations of mid-century modernist houses, designed by architects like Rudolph Schindler, Richard Neutra, John Lautner, and Craig Ellwood, as well as furniture designers Charles and Ray Eames, Paul Lásló, Paul Frankl, and Sam

Maloof, some of whom were also architects. These properties include the iconic Case Study Houses, famously initiated by John Entenza of *Arts & Architecture* magazine in 1945. They promoted the idea of California modernism, which featured less formality, with furniture made with new materials like fiberglass and plastic, as well as indoor-outdoor living. Today, designers like Darren Brown and Jamie Bush, and house restorer Mark Haddawy are renovating these newly popular mid-century houses, adding furniture of the period mixed with contemporary art and photography.

While the award-winning TV drama *Mad Men* was set in New York,

OPPOSITE: The interior of Frank Lloyd Wright's Hollyhock House was built between 1919 and 1921. This was his first Los Angeles commission. ABOVE, LEFT: The Adamson House, 1929, in Malibu, is a fine example of Spanish Colonial architecture. ABOVE, RIGHT: Tony Duquette was inspired by early Hollywood movies and designed film sets from the 1940s to the 1960s. Here he built his own fantasy buildings at Sortilegium, his ranch in Malibu.

13

it was filmed on soundstages in Los Angeles with Linda Wells heading the production team. The series starts in 1960, and the advertising agency and the homes of Don Draper were furnished with unerring accuracy of the period. While the interior design strove to reflect East Coast modernism, iconic LA houses and furniture stores, along with the world-famous Charles and Ray Eames House in Santa Monica, were significant influences. The same production team was responsible for Tom Ford's 2009 film *A Single Man*, which is set in 1962. The location was LA's Schaffer House, designed by John Lautner, and the interiors' accurate mid-century modern style was an inspiration to every designer who had just bought a modernist house.

In 1970, if you had movie star fame and money, your home was likely to be decorated in a French manner, almost indistinguishable from similar dwellings in Paris and New York. Eighteenth-century French furniture, now much less popular, commanded high prices, and stores opened in Los Angeles achieved iconic status. However, later in the 1970s designers like Sally Sirkin Lewis and

OPPOSITE, CLOCKWISE FROM TOP LEFT: The Ducommun House's glamorous interiors and furniture were designed by Tony Duquette in the mid-1960s—its dining and living rooms with a painting by Modigliani above the fireplace; Jean Howard's Hollywood Regency–style sitting room by William "Billy" Haines, and Betsy Bloomingdale's living room, also by Haines, which were both done in the late 1950s. ABOVE: Another view of the iconic Ducommun House by Duquette, showing his love of color, especially apricot pink and green.

Michael Taylor shifted the LA decorating world to a much younger, hipper look, with the inclusion of natural materials from the desert in their monochromatic interiors. A striking example of this style is the Beyer House, designed by John Lautner, which presides like a spaceship over the ocean at Malibu.

By the 1980s, LA decorating followed Michael Taylor's lead. Decorators such as Kalef Alaton, Val Arnold, and Steven Chase combined modern armchairs and sofas with slate tables, stone floors, and gilded French period furniture. At the same time, LA architects were experimenting with deconstructivism, breaking down the components of a building and reassembling them in new ways. The chief proponent was architect Frank Gehry, and his own house, designed in 1979, showed a radical rethinking of the Los Angeles house.

In the 1990s, designers Barbara Barry, Waldo Fernandez, and Michael S. Smith led the way, now almost entirely limiting the use of French period furniture, replacing it with English and Italian antiques, which went better with California stone and natural fibers and textures. Barry's vision of elegance was inspired by the furniture of the 1930s and 1940s, while Fernandez brought a more classical eye to the Michael Taylor school of natural materials. Smith

ABOVE: The 1959 Case Study House No. 21 (The Bailey House) by Pierre Koenig. OPPOSITE: John Lautner's 1971 Beyer House, decorated by Michael Taylor, is one of the most dramatic houses on the Malibu coast.

combined English-style upholstery with Italian period furniture and went on to decorate the Obama White House. Back in LA, designer Rose Tarlow's own house reached iconic status, with her monochromatic use of color and the rough texture of antique country furniture.

When the new millennium arrived, younger decorators began to make their mark. Martyn Lawrence Bullard came from England to be an actor in Hollywood but changed his profession to decorating. His love of glamour and overstated drama was like catnip to the entertainment industry, and his clients range from Sir Elton John to Cher—and include even

ABOVE: The Charles and Ray Eames Case Study House No. 8 from 1949. The couple were pioneers in the use of industrial materials. OPPOSITE, CLOCKWISE FROM TOP LEFT: The Schaffer House, by John Lautner, was also built in 1949. Frank Gehry's 1979 house with an iconic "stick" painting by Charles Arnoldi. The Gehry kitchen is one of the most published images of his house.

the Kardashians. Kelly Wearstler began her career with sophisticated 1950s-style designs for several hotels like the Avalon and the Viceroy. She soon expanded her range into a style that encompasses mid-century modern with a very eclectic contemporary eye. Mary McDonald came from the fashion industry; her work reflects a rich understanding of fabrics and textiles. Her houses are beautifully crafted with a strong color sense and style. Kerry Joyce's calm modernism was also influential, and his interiors continued the tradition set by Kalef Alaton of stylish comfort in monochromatic tones.

By the 2020s, new interior designers and architects were in full swing. The Archers, a collective spearheaded by Richard Petit, bring a strong modern Italian vibe to decorating, while Commune Design, who describe themselves as a community of like-minded architects, interior designers, graphic designers, artisans, and builders, have created their own definition of California cool. David Netto is not only a sophisticated decorator, immersed in the history of craft traditions, but also an accomplished author and design writer, while Pamela Shamshiri of Studio Shamshiri is known for her refined bohemian aesthetic.

OPPOSITE, CLOCKWISE FROM TOP LEFT: A Sally Sirkin Lewis sitting room from the 1970s, Barbara Barry's dining room decorated in the 1980s, Mary McDonald's 2005 tented room, and Rose Tarlow's guest bedroom from her 1990 Bel Air house. ABOVE: Martyn Lawrence Bullard's living room from around 2013.

These days there is no longer a distinctive California "look" unlike the mid-century modernist period of the 1950s. Influences are gleaned from all over the world, and LA interiors now feature a mix of furnishings and art. With the declining reach of decorating magazines, interior design has become powered by Instagram and stores that sell a diverse mix of furniture, both old and new, inspiring decorators and homeowners alike. Stores like Hollywood at Home, Pucci, Blackman Cruz, Indigo Seas, Lee Stanton, Galerie Half, Obsolete, and JF Chen do more than reflect the current tastes and styles—they set the trends with their curated mix of furniture, fabrics, room layouts, and art.

Many architects, designers, and decorators have set to work reviving the often historically protected houses of the twentieth century, a trend that began with early design enthusiasts with deep pockets like film producer Joel Silver, who in 1984 bought the Storer House, designed by Frank Lloyd Wright, followed by actor Diane Keaton, who renovated a house by Frank Lloyd Wright's son Lloyd Wright in 1992. Homeowners in Los Angeles today continue to renovate and restore houses, making them more efficient and at the same time more personal. This book surveys some of the most inspiring examples from over a hundred years of decorating and design in Los Angeles. We have divided these homes into two categories—Living with Art and Design and Los Angeles Modern.

OPPOSITE, TOP: Kelly Wearstler's house in Trousdale from the early 2000s. OPPOSITE, BOTTOM: A calm, orderly sitting room by Kerry Joyce, decorated in 1999. ABOVE, LEFT: The ever-changing and eclectic Blackman Cruz store. ABOVE, RIGHT: JF Chen's new shop on Highland Avenue.

PART I
LIVING WITH ART AND DESIGN

Los Angeles living spaces feature a cosmopolitan mix of furnishings and art. Eclecticism is a common thread running through these interiors.

OPPOSITE: Frank Gehry's vast *Octopus* hangs from the ceiling of the Beverly Hills home of art writer Hunter Drohojowska-Philp and musician David Philp. The figurative paintings above and below the stair landing are by Chris Finley, while the geometric artwork is by Jim Isermann.

VILLA VALLOMBROSA
WHITLEY HEIGHTS

The Venetian-style Villa Vallombrosa overlooks a tiny hidden valley in Whitley Heights, a residential neighborhood developed in the 1920s to recreate the Mediterranean spirit of hillside villages in France, Spain, and Italy. The villa typifies the element of fantasy for which Hollywood became famous in the 1920s and '30s. With its curved facade and single long window like an exclamation point, it evokes a Venetian palazzo or a small villa in Tuscany.

DECORATED BY ANNIE KELLY

About twenty years ago, my husband, photographer Tim Street-Porter, and I bought this historic property from friends who had done much of the original restoration. From a broad terrace above the street, the front door opens onto a tiny hall with a Gothic arch, from which tunnel-like stairs curve theatrically upward and into the twenty-foot-high sitting room on the *piano nobile*, or main floor. Here, aged milk-coffee-colored walls meet the ceiling in a soft cove, giving the room a sensation of limitless height. A carved stone fireplace anchors the room beneath a gilded Louis Philippe mirror flanked by a pair of nineteenth-century sconces.

The villa is essentially one large room that anchors the rest of the house. It is built into the hillside, and at the rear is a central enclosed courtyard with an outdoor fireplace set into the wall at one side. Much of the furniture that we found for the house is French, Italian, Syrian, or Turkish, and was bought from various antiques shops and auction houses in Los Angeles. The artwork is mainly from friends: Californian artists like Ed Ruscha, Dan McCleary, Konstantin Kakanias, James hd Brown, and Cosmas and Damian Brown, as well as Billy Al Bengston and Charles Arnoldi.

The smaller sitting room owes a lot to the extraordinary Tony Duquette. He suggested

OPPOSITE: An eighteenth-century English portrait, flanked by a pair of nineteenth-century French chairs, hangs on a cutwork Egyptian textile at the back of the twenty-foot-high-ceilinged sitting room.

and supplied the mirror for this room, to reflect the courtyard garden outside. The twin pagodas flanking the Empire chest of drawers came from his workshop.

Villa Vallombrosa has a rich history. In 1931, two years after the house was built, the costume designer Adrian moved in. Photographs in a recent book on his work show the dramatic Hollywood Regency–style decoration of the sitting room, and a memoir by Mercedes de Acosta mentions an evening she spent there with Greta Garbo. This proximity to Garbo drew photographer Cecil Beaton to the villa. In his memoirs, he exclaimed: "I would have a house like this if I lived in Hollywood."

ABOVE: An original wrought-iron lantern hangs over Villa Vallombrosa's front door. OPPOSITE: The gunite front facade is slightly curved, with a thirteen-foot-tall front window opening onto a Juliet balcony. The house is designated as a Los Angeles Historic-Cultural Monument. FOLLOWING SPREAD: The double-height sitting room is furnished with nineteenth-century furniture from Italy, France, Syria, and Turkey. The three chairs and a cushion are upholstered in Carmania from Peter Dunham Textiles.

OPPOSITE: The Syrian armoire was bought locally at auction. The nineteenth-century French chair is upholstered in Queen Anne by Robert Kime. ABOVE: A nineteenth-century armchair next to the fireplace is upholstered with Carmania from Peter Dunham Textiles.

ABOVE, CLOCKWISE FROM LEFT: The small gilded lion was bought in the Zona Rosa in Mexico City; the plaster pagoda was a gift from Tony Duquette; the thirteen-foot-tall front sitting room windows overlooking the street are draped with linen; and in front of an eighteenth-century French print is a pot by Los Angeles artist David Lloyd. OPPOSITE: The villa's enclosed interior courtyard viewed from the main bedroom balcony. A copa d'oro vine climbs down the walls.

A self-portrait by the fashion photographer Baron Adolph de Meyer, taken in front of the sitting room fireplace when he lived here in the 1940s, now hangs in the same room. Another colorful tenant was Edward James, a great patron of surrealist art, and possibly the model for Sebastian Flyte in Evelyn Waugh's *Brideshead Revisited*, who moved into a remote corner of the Mexican jungle where he built Las Pozas, an inscrutable folly of towers and spires. An example of the enduring Los Angeles preoccupation with creating a fantasy environment, the Villa Vallombrosa lives on in the same spirit in which it was designed.

OPPOSITE: The smaller sitting room has a chinoiserie theme, with a collection of Chinese ancestor paintings and reverse-glass paintings. The secretary desk came from Coveney Manor, the Street-Porter family house in England.
ABOVE: A print by Billy Al Bengston accompanies a seventeenth-century portrait hanging above the sofa. On the left is a Chinese statue of Guan Yin. The June Street armchairs, bought at Hollyhock, are upholstered in Schumacher's Chavant Paisley. Tony Duquette provided the mirror, which reflects the courtyard.

ABOVE: A Portuguese bed dominates the main bedroom. The bed fabrics are from Les Indiennes. Above the bed on the left is a painting by James hd Brown, flanked by a pair of reliquaries from Tony Duquette. On the far right is a still life by Dan McCleary. OPPOSITE: A nineteenth-century French daybed sits opposite the bed; the damask cushion fabrics are from Fortuny, and the gilded mirror was bought at JF Chen.

ABOVE, LEFT: The downstairs bedroom drawing is by James hd Brown. ABOVE RIGHT: Two works by Ed Ruscha hang above a piece by Pippa Garner. To the left is a Ganzer stand by Jim Ganzer. OPPOSITE: The pillowcases on the bed are from Les Indiennes. On the wall to the left is a watercolor by Peter Shire, and on the opposing wall are works by Dan McCleary, Magnus Edensvard, Ed Ruscha, and Charles Arnoldi, among others.

41

LEE STANTON
LAGUNA BEACH

If you were looking for the perfect hideout in Laguna Beach, you couldn't do better than antiquarian Lee Stanton's treasure-filled house on the coast, overlooking a small sandy bay. It is almost impossible to find along a strip of shops and take-out restaurants; you drive through what looks like a parking lot to a pair of tall iron gates that give no clue to what lies beyond. It's a surprise to discover a long tree-lined drive that transports you down to what looks like an English manor house, which was bought and reworked by Stanton over twenty-five years ago.

A mainstay of Los Angeles's design community, Stanton's elegant eponymous store is centrally placed in the heart of the decorating world on La Cienega Boulevard in West Hollywood. He began his career in the late eighties with a shop in San Louis Obispo, a picturesque small town on the south coast of California, but with its success Stanton soon moved to the bigger market of Los Angeles. Stanton enjoys retreating to the beach after a week's work in town. While there are two other floors, reached by an 1840s French spiral staircase, the upper floor is a guest suite, while the lower floor contains a small apartment; Stanton lives mainly on what could be considered the main floor, or *piano nobile*.

Climbing up the stone steps in the entry tower, lit by two lanterns bought from the Duchess of Windsor estate auction, the stairs open directly into a paneled dining room. Here, Directoire dining chairs encircle an English table, and the Italian chandelier overhead shows how Stanton enjoys pairing Italian furniture with English pieces. This space leads into a main sitting room, with a distracting ocean view. We could be anywhere on the Mediterranean; it's hard to believe we are in a surfing beach town.

The main bedroom also enjoys an ocean view with its regal Italian Empire bed, complete with built-in candlesticks, overlooking a Louis XVI daybed up against the window. The neoclassical mood continues in the dressing room, with its pale wood closets and dark marble surfaces. Even the kitchen feels like you have traveled through a portal to France, with its stone floors, nineteenth-century wall clock, and a painted wall frieze depicting scenes from *Paul et Virginie*.

OPPOSITE: **An eighteenth-century French oak spiral staircase leads to guest rooms on the third floor. Lee Stanton placed a nineteenth-century bust of Brutus at the base of the stairs.**

Every piece of furniture and decorative object has a story; Stanton finds everything in Europe and the UK, often at antiques markets and fairs. Like needles in a haystack, each piece has a particular style, line, or story that appeals to him. Sometimes, although rarely, he sells something from this house at his Los Angeles store or at his new shop in Montecito, called Private Stash.

Even after spending thirty years off and on in Laguna Beach, Stanton never tires of the contrast to his workweek in town. He enjoys the peace of the distant ocean horizon and the comfort of being surrounded by his treasured furniture collections.

ABOVE: A pair of early nineteenth-century Italian chairs, a leather-topped small table, and a nineteenth-century French sofa sit in front of a sunny window. OPPOSITE: An early nineteenth-century French officer's piece of furniture made of apple wood is on display in the main sitting room.

ABOVE, LEFT: An eighteenth-century oak chest of drawers is topped with antique sculptural stone elements. ABOVE, RIGHT: French Directoire chairs encircle an English dining table. A nineteenth-century Italian chandelier hangs above it. OPPOSITE, LEFT: The view from the rustic English kitchen table is up the driveway. An Italian tole and crystal chandelier hangs above the table, where Empire tole cachepots and an Arts and Crafts brass bowl have been set. OPPOSITE, RIGHT: One of a pair of eighteenth-century painted Directoire cupboards is topped with a collection of nineteenth-century carved wood architectural elements. A nineteenth-century seascape hangs above it. FOLLOWING SPREAD: The French country kitchen is fitted with stone floors and a nineteenth-century wall clock. The refrigerator is Sub-Zero, the sink fittings are from Rohl, and the range is by Viking.

RIGHT: The main bedroom with its Louis XVI daybed has views out to the ocean and a small sandy beach. The painted eighteenth-century cupboard is from Italy.

ABOVE: The nineteenth-century Italian Empire main bed with built-in candleholders has a sea view. The walls are hung with a collection of ocean-themed paintings.
OPPOSITE: The main bathroom has a cement and stone tile floor; a French lantern hangs above a French Empire marble-top pedestal table.

JOEL CHEN

HANCOCK PARK

For decades Joel Chen has been a formidable tastemaker in Los Angeles. His store, JF Chen, has tended to focus on furniture of the twentieth century. However, the shop always looks and feels like a living museum of contemporary design and decoration and is doubly attractive since everything is for sale.

Chen lives with his wife, Margaret, in Hancock Park in an English Tudor–style house, which they bought over thirty years ago. The area was developed in the 1920s and is relatively untouched by development, containing some majestic Spanish Colonial, neoclassical, and European-style houses with generous front lawns.

From the street, the house blends in with its patrician neighbors who have no clue to the treasures within. Inside, you find extraordinary and rare furniture from all over the world. An elegant ornamental stair rail leads to the second-floor rooms, where Chen has an office as well as several bedrooms. This is where the couple raised their two daughters, Bianca and Fiona. In the two living areas, Chen has assembled a very eclectic collection of furniture, linked by color and materials, if not by period or origin. These rooms reflect his global sense of style—he mixes Italian period furniture with Chinese objects in wood, bone, and lacquer; Portuguese cabinets; and stainless-steel chairs, which all somehow fit together, linked by his sense of connoisseurship.

At a nearby exhibition space on Highland Avenue, Chen introduces artists and specific furnishings collections to the LA design and art worlds. He has long helped shape tastes in Los Angeles—especially with his store's eclectically curated mix of art and design.

OPPOSITE: The entryway with stairs leading up to the second floor has a custom ornate metal railing.

OPPOSITE: The sitting room has a hand-painted Japanese screen from the nineteenth-century Meiji period featuring cranes. A scholar's rock sits on the console table. ABOVE: Contemporary Danish chairs by Preben Fabricius and Jørgen Kastholm accompany a matching table set in front of a pair of eighteenth-century Italian columns originally from Hearst Castle. FOLLOWING SPREAD: A second seating area with a red leather sofa in front of a pair of Japanese screens overlooks the back garden. On the pedestal is an Italian Nubian figure. Sitting on the steel coffee table, bought from Ellen DeGeneres, is an animal-shaped Song dynasty bronze incense burner. In front of it is a Seagull chair and ottoman.

ABOVE: Another contemporary seating group with 1980s stainless-steel chairs by Krueck and Sexton architects is accompanied by a wood buffet cupboard. OPPOSITE: A tabletop featuring an eighteenth-century Chinese eunuch figure seated on a Japanese root pedestal is in front of a Japanese screen. FOLLOWING SPREAD: The eclectic main sitting room features a coffee table by George Nakashima, a painting by Charles Safford, and a Laverne International sofa from the office of architect Minoru Yamasaki.

PAGE 64, CLOCKWISE FROM TOP LEFT: Garlic-shaped wooden elements and a collection of white ceramics from designers such as Ettore Sottsass sit on an antique Portuguese cabinet; a close-up of a hand-painted Japanese screen from the nineteenth-century Meiji period featuring cranes is behind a scholar's rock that has been placed on the console table; and a rare brass stool by T. H.Robsjohn-Gibbings. PAGE 65, CLOCKWISE FROM TOP LEFT: A Copenhagen chair by Voltelen and Vodder; a Carrara marble bust of Juliette Récamier; a primitive carved chair with leopard skin fabric seat, and a mid-century modern mirror. RIGHT: Chen's upstairs office includes a bamboo chair by Jeff Dayu Shi.

JEAN-LOUIS DENIOT
WEST HOLLYWOOD

International designers are often attracted to the freedom and space of Los Angeles. Some, like fashion designers Tom Ford and Jeremy Scott, have moved here more or less permanently, while others visit throughout the year, like decorator Jean-Louis Deniot, who has been a part-time resident for nearly twenty years. This leading designer works all over the world and owns homes in France and Morocco, as well as the United States; his decorating tends to reflect all these influences. Deniot enjoys the light and stylistic eclecticism of Los Angeles and finds it a retreat from the pressure of his international design business.

This Tudor-style house in the Hollywood Hills with echoes of a Spanish Revival style was built in the 1930s. When he acquired the home, Deniot's main concern was to increase its size, which he did in two ways. First, he added a dining room below a new main bedroom and bathroom. Second, with the skill of garden designer Scott Shrader, Deniot created a series of seven outdoor rooms in difficult steep hillside conditions. Shrader worked wonders in such unforgiving terrain; these extra spaces considerably enlarged the living area of the whole property.

One of the main reasons Deniot was attracted to this house is the high cathedral ceiling of the main living space, which he enhanced with an out-of-scale seventeenth-century Spanish chandelier and a pair of large indoor palm trees. Deniot enjoys playing with scale and period—this space also includes an early American eighteenth-century armchair covered in new Indonesian raffia.

Under the palm trees, he positioned armchairs that he designed for Baker Furniture and added a Tony Duquette lamp on the mantelpiece. Beautiful custom-embroidered curtains from Jean-François Lesage hang in the front windows, elegantly framing a dramatic view of the city. The house contains a mix of different periods of furniture, centered on 1940s pieces from Jacques Adnet,

OPPOSITE: The exterior of Jean-Louis Deniot's 1920s Tudor-style house with a tower in West Hollywood incorporates Spanish Revival—style elements.

but also furnishings from all over the world, including Morocco, Africa, Turkey, and naturally, France.

In the dining room, Deniot hung a large, gilded mirror by Tony Duquette above the fireplace, and created a white plaster chandelier to hang over the Piet Hein Eek dining table, which sports candlesticks by the design duo Garouste & Bonetti.

In the library, a T. H. Robsjohn-Gibbings daybed separates the space from the new dining room. Deniot designed the bronze and parchment

ABOVE: The curved staircase in the entry leads up to the bedrooms. Underneath sits an eighteenth-century English armchair, covered in raffia fabric from Indonesia, next to a 1940s *guerdon* by André Groult. OPPOSITE: The sitting room is dominated by a pair of fishtail palm trees; flanking the fireplace are matching chairs designed by Deniot for Baker. The coffee table in straw marquetry is from Lison de Caunes, and the gold leaf Capsule stool is by Hervé van der Straeten. A lamp by Tony Duquette sits on the mantelpiece.

ABOVE, LEFT: The seventeenth-century Spanish chandelier in the sitting room has custom raffia shades by Anne Sokolsky. ABOVE, RIGHT: In the dining room, a nineteenth-century Ethiopian shield anchors an arrangement on a French table from the 1940s, which includes an American mid-century straw and rope lamp and an eighteenth-century terra-cotta vase from Morocco. OPPOSITE, LEFT: A view into the dining room, which features a mirror by Tony Duquette. OPPOSITE, RIGHT: A pair of Garouste & Bonetti bronze candle-sticks sits on a table by Piet Hein Eek. The oak dining chairs are from Jacques Adnet.

RIGHT: The library's seating includes a daybed by T. H. Robsjohn-Gibbings and a sofa by Deniot for Baker covered in a Nobilis fabric. PAGE 76: In the guest room, a Tony Duquette shell chandelier hangs above the nineteenth-century Etruscan-style bronze colonial bed. The Moroccan curtains are custom made. PAGE 77: The main bathroom mirror is designed by Karl Springer; the bathtub is from Aston Matthews.

bookcase, and added the sofa, which is part of his line of furniture for Baker. Upstairs, a small guest bedroom occupies the tower where a sparkling Tony Duquette chandelier made with abalone shells overlooks a nineteenth-century Etruscan-style bronze colonial bed.

Deniot added the main bedroom, which, thanks to the slope of the hill, leads outside to various garden rooms. He copied the existing ceilings to fit in with the rest of the house and commissioned a custom chandelier from Marie Christophe. The designer turned the focus of the house toward the view, and at night, the city spreads out like a carpet of lights from the front windows.

OPPOSITE, CLOCKWISE, FROM TOP LEFT: A detail of the nineteenth-century Etruscan-style bronze colonial bed in the guest room; Tony Duquette abalone shell chandelier; a Murano Glass globe lamp; the main bathroom's mirror from Karl Springer. ABOVE: The main bedroom custom chandelier was designed by Marie Christophe. A bench by Jean-Michel Frank sits at the foot of the bed. FOLLOWING SPREAD: The garden sitting area, designed by Scott Shrader, includes wrought-iron armchairs from Cleo Baldon, and an outdoor fireplace by Shrader Design with a vintage convex mirror.

GARRETT HUNTER
AND MICHAEL LANDRUM'S
CHATEAU X
HOLLYWOOD

Whitley Heights in the Hollywood Hills is famous for its celebrity history—classic film stars like Bette Davis and Gloria Swanson lived in this Mediterranean-style hillside neighborhood, conveniently close to the movie studios in nearby Burbank and Hollywood. Creative partners, designer Garrett Hunter and architect Michael Landrum were looking to move out of Texas during the pandemic, and considered relocating to Los Angeles, where both had worked on design projects in the past. Ending up in the middle of old Hollywood wasn't necessarily part of the plan, but the design duo came across this charming two-story 1930s Hollywood Regency house, which became a perfect pied-à-terre as well as a great location to introduce and showcase their experimental gallery and showroom for their furniture company, Tienda X. They move their inventory to each house they occupy. "It's a movable, ever-evolving store," says Hunter.

Each of them came to the table with certain collecting passions. Landrum's are Mexican craft and folk art, seventeenth-century Italian and Spanish furniture, and a love of the 1920s and 1930s, while Hunter is passionate about early-to-mid-twentieth-century California furnishings and later iconic twentieth-century design. Their strength lies in a blended mix of the two that manages to be both streamlined and eclectic at the same time.

OPPOSITE: On the front terrace of this Hollywood Regency–style house is a Richard Schultz prototype metal chair.

The business partners speedily filled the nearly 2,000-square-foot house, which they promptly named Chateau X, with containers of furniture from Brooklyn, Austin, and Houston and opened the doors to clients and friends. In the main living room, they hung vintage Fortuny fabric curtains, which unexpectedly were a perfect fit, added a resin "Ginkgo" chair of their own design, and twentieth-century French metal armchairs. They moved the dining area into this room, choosing to repurpose the former dining room into a second, more intimate sitting room—and hung a large painting by Los Angeles artist Louis Eisner.

The quirky style of the architecture, with its randomly placed Gothic arches, Louis XIV–style marble fireplace, and small wood-paneled library goes well with the eclectic collection of Tienda X art and furniture. This includes pieces of their own design, a spin-off that they call Studio X, and as Hunter adds, "We always did intend to make our own furniture."

RIGHT: The living room's twentieth-century red metal armchairs sit opposite a Ginkgo chair by Studio X. Vintage Fortuny curtains hang in the windows; above the fireplace is a painting by Alfred Henry Maurer. The coffee table is by Philip and Kelvin LaVerne.

ABOVE: In the dining area, a Thomas Hucker table is surrounded by an eclectic collection of chairs. The large painting is by Louis Eisner. Steps lead down to the main bedroom. OPPOSITE, CLOCKWISE FROM TOP RIGHT: Seen from the entry, the dining area features a Rosario Murabito leather painting. The main bedroom downstairs is furnished with a Japanese art deco bed; a Peruvian throw serves as a backdrop for a painting by Melesio Galván. In the upstairs bedroom, a photograph by Dash Snow hangs in front of a seventeenth-century Flemish tapestry. The drawings are by Seth Alverson; the mercury glass lamps are from Mike Diaz. A collection of pots sits on a seventeenth-century Vargueño desk in the living room.

MAYER RUS
SILVER LAKE

You might be forgiven for thinking that writer and editor Mayer Rus is the ultimate design maven. After all, he has spent years writing about design and decoration for a range of national newspapers and magazines, including *The New York Times*, *The Wall Street Journal*, *Elle Decor*, and *Artforum*, as well as a stint at *Interior Design* magazine. Now based in Los Angeles, Rus is currently the West Coast editor of top-in-its-field *Architectural Digest* magazine. There is not much he hasn't seen—visiting and writing about houses owned by most of the Kardashian family, as well as homes of celebrities like Robert Downey Jr., Gwyneth Paltrow, and Ricky Martin. However, when it comes to his own house, his choices are wildly eclectic and quite personal.

Given his experience working in the Los Angeles design world, it is interesting that he chose this small house overlooking Silver Lake rather than anywhere else in the vast and rambling city. As well as enjoying the sunsets over the lake, the house sits high up on a large lot of land with views on all sides of the property. Perhaps this is why it was built as a hunting cabin in 1908, although it has been greatly altered over the years. The house is compact, at just under nine hundred square feet, with a small separate one-room guesthouse, and filled with the history of the past ten years—with nothing purposefully reminding Rus of his past life in New York.

Rus discovered the cottage while he was working for the *L.A. Times* as the magazine's design and culture editor and rented it for the first few years. When he left the magazine, he decided not to return to New York and bought the property to make a commitment to his new hometown.

During the past ten years, Rus has sensitively remodeled the small house. He reworked the bathroom and kitchen and added French doors and a bathroom to upgrade

OPPOSITE: Two busts, including a Trudon Napoleon candle, sit together on a Black Forest—style nineteenth-century wood wall bracket.

ABOVE: A nineteenth-century bison head overlooks the living room, furnished with a sofa from Commune that Linus is enjoying and a suede armchair from Escarpa. A Gaetano Pesce resin vase is next to the television. OPPOSITE: A corner of the living room shows how a desk, a Noguchi Akari paper lamp, an Eero Saarinen chair, and a reworked Swiss-style chair can all mix happily together.

RIGHT: The guesthouse
screen that once hung in
an Idaho post office
depicts rustic scenes; in
front of it is a blue
cabinet from IKEA, and
on the left is a rare
Noguchi paper lamp.

RIGHT: The bedroom bed-spread is taken from Burt Reynolds's *Cosmopolitan* magazine spread of 1972; the wall hanging is a Chinese propaganda scene featuring Chairman Mao.

the guesthouse. The garden has been replanted with suitable dry climate plants, and despite its far-reaching views, it still feels to him like a tree house nestled in the green.

Steps up from the street, and past a terrace overlooking the lake view, the house opens immediately to a living space, where a large stuffed bison head confronts the visitor. A consummate smoker, Rus's walls are tobacco stained, which is exactly how he likes them. Linus the dog can often be found on the L-shaped sofa from his friends at Commune, which is near a comfortable suede armchair from Escarpa for B&B Italia.

Rus has contributed many essays to books by designers including Richard Shapiro, Atelier AM, Lee Ledbetter, and many others, so it is only natural that they have piled up in his bedroom, where an impressive bedspread depicts Burt Reynolds's iconic nude *Cosmopolitan* magazine cover spread of 1972. Outside the back door sits the small guesthouse, where Rus added large French doors to take advantage of the urban views from the house. Here, he has continued the hunting lodge theme with four large wall panels depicting rustic scenes once hanging in an Idaho post office. Surrounded by his own design world souvenirs, it must be a relief for the once labeled "Testy Tastemaker" to be able to return to his own stylish microcosm here in Silver Lake after all the heady glamour of his chosen career.

RIGHT: An outdoor table, laid with a collection of ceramic pieces accumulated during Rus's travels, overlooks Silver Lake.

Mirrors and Windows Szarkowski The Museum of Modern Art, New York

LAMPUGNANI ENCYCLOPEDIA OF 20TH-CENTURY ARCHITECTURE ABRAMS

THE MACHINE AGE THE BROOKLYN MUSEUM ABRAMS

HINES IRVING GILL AND THE ARCHITECT

WILLIAM BRICE REVELA

am Architecture

Frankl and Modern

REMAINING SEATS

Western Ranch H

SANTA FE

311

Abrams

TIM STREET-PORTER'S STUDIO
HOLLYWOOD

The corner of Hollywood and Vine occupies a special place in Hollywood history. During the golden age of Hollywood filmmaking, it was known as the heart of the film and entertainment industry, and during the 1930s a popular radio station made this corner a household name across America with its broadcasts "Live from Hollywood and Vine." Today, it's the center of the Hollywood Walk of Fame—an avenue of pavement stars begun in 1958, which continues to add more stars every year.

Photographer Tim Street-Porter was searching for a studio and happened across the redevelopment of the historic 1929 Equitable Building, originally designed by architect Aleck

**DECORATED BY
ANNIE KELLY**

Curlett in what was considered a Gothic deco style. An apartment was available overlooking this iconic Hollywood corner. As part of the adaptive reuse of the commercial building, the 1,200-square-foot space was designated historic, which meant that the rooms retained the original Raymond Chandler–like office doors and were to remain carpeted for reasons best known to the developers.

To showcase Street-Porter's work, the author decided to keep the color palette modern and monochromatic, with white walls and glossy lacquered furniture. The loftlike ceiling had been painted black; she immediately resprayed it white. Into this new space Street-Porter moved his archives and hung a changing exhibition of his color photography.

OPPOSITE: A collection of architecture books and childhood trains and cars occupies a corner of Tim Street-Porter's studio bookcase. The historic building, which once housed the Bank of Hollywood, is designated a Los Angeles Historic-Cultural Monument.

ABOVE: Street-Porter's glass collection, found in flea markets and stores from France, Connecticut, Sydney, Santa Barbara, and Los Angeles, enlivens a window overlooking Hollywood Boulevard. OPPOSITE: A chair and cushions from Martyn Lawrence Bullard are part of the furnishings of the main seating area. The artwork is a Street-Porter photograph of the now destroyed Pan Pacific theater. FOLLOWING SPREAD: The main workspace has been kept chiefly in monochromatic tones to serve as a backdrop to Street-Porter's color photographs. The desk is from West Elm. A vase by Peter Shire sits on a pedestal table gifted to Street-Porter by fellow photographer Firooz Zahedi.

A 1970s chrome-and-glass dining table bought at auction doubles as a worktable and is surrounded by transparent chairs found at IKEA. The main living space is one long room the width of the front wing of this double-facade building. Street-Porter's collection of twentieth-century glass found at flea markets from Sydney to New Milford, Connecticut, fills the many windowsills with glowing transparent shapes and colors. A pair of cushions from decorator Martyn Lawrence Bullard was a studio-warming present. Bullard also provided the white leather Rive Gauche club chair from his furniture line; however, much of the rest of the furniture was found at affordable West Elm and IKEA.

Street-Porter switched to digital photography nearly fifteen years ago, but over the years he had accumulated a vast inventory of film, which fills rows of white storage bins along one wall, topped with a display of the books he has written and photographed during his long career. A red Royal typewriter decorates a desk nearby, an homage to artist Ed Ruscha's 1967 art book *Royal Road Test*.

The apartment has extensive views along Hollywood Boulevard, where on a clear day the Getty Museum can be seen on a far-off hilltop, as well as buildings down much of Vine Street. Two other historic buildings remain on this corner—the Taft Building, where Charlie Chaplin was rumored to have a production office, and the 1927 Broadway Department Store, now redeveloped as apartments. Hollywood has changed a lot since the golden days of filmmaking; however, Street-Porter's building is filled with musicians and producers, and Netflix currently has more than 800,000 square feet of production space in Hollywood—so the dream continues.

OPPOSITE: In another corner of the live-work loft is a 1970s chrome-and-glass table found at auction, transparent chairs from IKEA, and a photograph by Street-Porter of the iconic Los Angeles City Hall. This room looks down onto the famous corner of Hollywood and Vine.

RIGHT: Street-Porter's library features books on photography and architecture, many of which contain his own photographs. Along the top of the bookcase is a small selection of the books photographed and written by him and author Annie Kelly.
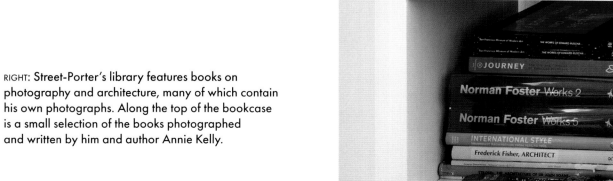

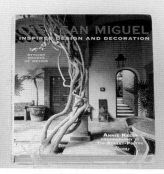

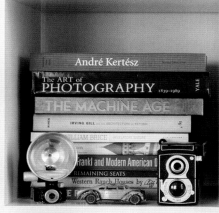

THE ARNOLDI HOUSE

MALIBU

The beginning of a late twentieth-century art world movement unique to Los Angeles sprang from a creative group of artists, sculptors, and architects with roots in the 1960s. Charles (Chuck) Arnoldi belongs to this evolving West Coast scene that includes the architect Frank Gehry, artist Ed Ruscha, sculptor Larry Bell, and ceramicist Ken Price. Centered in Venice, California, many of these artists created studios for themselves that included innovative design ideas.

Several years later and farther up the coast in Malibu, Arnoldi has now designed a home for himself and his family that represents his work, his interests, and his collections. His elegantly restrained modern house dates back to over twenty-five years ago, when Arnoldi designed it to fit a deep lot overlooking Little Dume Beach. Arnoldi has a history of collaborating on loft and studio developments with Gehry, who made a few suggestions; however, Arnoldi has a strong sense of space and light of his own that shows in his artwork and in much of the furniture, which he also designed.

DESIGNED BY CHARLES ARNOLDI

The house is basically a box with big glass windows on two sides, effectively making it transparent so the ocean can be seen through the building as soon as you drive onto the property. Exposed to the sea, it has an elemental feel, with its walls of troweled concrete and marine-grade plywood woodwork. The central living room has a twenty-foot-high ceiling, anchored by a tall chimneypiece hung with a painting from Arnoldi's *Potatoes* series, where both fire and water can be seen in one take during cold winter days

OPPOSITE: Charles Arnoldi designed the dining table, which looks out through the open door to the Pacific Ocean, and the stick chandelier above. A rare bronze by Frank Gehry sits in the center of the table.

and nights. Arnoldi and his wife, Katie, have raised two children in bedrooms on one side of this light-filled cube, while their bedroom and library lead via a staircase to its other side.

Throughout the house, Arnoldi has hung works by fellow artists who have been longtime friends. Pottery by the late Ken Price, an early Frank Gehry pale fish sculpture, and a classic work by Billy Al Bengston are intermingled with Indigenous art and artifacts to reveal a consistency of vision that reflects his involvement with nature and his art. A large luminous shark painting by his daughter, Natalie, an artist and marine

ABOVE: A fish sculpture by Frank Gehry tops a wood pedestal in the dining area.
OPPOSITE: In the living room, a work from Arnoldi's *Potatoes* series hangs on the tall fireplace chimney. Arnoldi also designed the coffee table.

ABOVE: On the wall opposite the fireplace hangs a painting by Arnoldi's daughter, Natalie. He designed the leather armchairs. OPPOSITE: In the main bedroom, a large moving window on ball bearings has a view of the living room and the hand-troweled concrete floor below.

RIGHT: The dining area's table with Charles and Ray Eames chairs overlooks the ocean and a sculptural cactus garden designed by Arnoldi.

biologist, dominates the back wall of the living room.

Arnoldi designed a large moving window on ball bearings that is constructed like a piece of sculpture, overlooking the hand-troweled concrete floors below. Here, in the dining area, sits a vast table with an elemental chandelier hung above it; both were designed by the artist. This room looks out to a cactus garden that Arnoldi planted; it does double duty as a living sculpture garden. An outdoor dining gazebo looks over the ocean; made of logs, it continues the organic feel of the garden and references Arnoldi's original works in wood.

OPPOSITE: The see-through house is basically a box. Big glass windows on both sides provide views of Little Dume Beach. ABOVE: Arnoldi designed a solid wood gazebo for outdoor ocean-side dining.

JORGENSEN HOUSE

HOLLYWOOD HILLS

The Jorgensen House was built in 1980 and planned by architect Frederick Fisher as a conceptual response to the wildfires that had recently destroyed a number of houses in Southern California. He intended this studio to appear like a relic of a recent burned-out ruin. Commissioned by then owner, screenwriter Kim Jorgensen, it was intended to be a freestanding building below the main house. Jorgensen needed a place to write, and this simple Japanese-inspired ridge-beam building, with jetliner views all over Los Angeles, was an ideal location.

Fast-forward forty years, and the new owners, producer Jonah Disend and sculptor David Altmejd, realized that this small iconic building at the bottom of their property needed renovation. They wanted to do it right, without losing the iconic 1980s feel of the space, so they brought in the well-known design company the Archers, spearheaded by award-winning lead designer Richard Petit. After careful consultation with Fisher, they reorganized the interior and cleaned up the exterior. Petit realized that this building, which stands exposed on a hillside prow, has its own stressful climate, and thus needed to be reinforced against the elements. Over the course of three years, they repointed the concrete blocks, and redid the roof by removing the red tile, which was not on the original plans, replacing it with Bonderized steel—galvanized metal put through a phosphate bath, giving it a dull gray finish.

DESIGNED BY FREDERICK FISHER, RENOVATED BY THE ARCHERS

OPPOSITE: The exterior concrete block facade by architect Frederick Fisher was cleaned and repointed. PAGE 120: A bright green vase by Gaetano Pesce sits next to the enameled blue front door. PAGE 121: In the dining area there are chairs by Marcel Wanders, a VIP Table by Dirk van der Kooij, and a plexiglass hanging lamp from Vico Magistretti in Italy.

They created the kitchen and enclosed a powder room to make a more functional bathroom. Project lead Tyler Polich, helped by Aimee Sun, also supervised the reworking of the outdoor spaces and linked the project with the two other upper buildings through a series of tinted concrete steps and landings.

Inside, the main living space has been furnished with an eclectic mix of objects—inspired by an earlier photograph of the interior that featured a Barbarian chair by Garouste & Bonetti. The designers brought in a cof-

ABOVE: The coffee table is by Élisabeth Garouste the throw on the sofa is from Denis Colomb and the table lamp is by Gae Aulenti. OPPOSITE: For this early photo taken by Street-Porter when the house was built in 1980, he brought in his own Garouste & Bonetti Barbarian chair.

RIGHT: The design team from the Archers added this new kitchen while preserving the original composition of the concrete walls.

fee table by the same designers, as well as a custom swinging sofa by Élisabeth Garouste. The signature-colored wall tiles were carefully cleaned and restored, and the front door painted a rich blue enamel. In the dining area, a set of Marcel Wanders VIP dining chairs surround a colorful round table. Downstairs the designers created a walk-in wardrobe and writing space behind the bed wall and warmed the space up with a natural fiber rug. This studio with its iconic views over Los Angeles will last into the next century now that the Archers have successfully restored it.

OPPOSITE: **The existing main bathroom was restored.** ABOVE: **The designers created a work space behind the bed, designed by the Archers, in the main bedroom. The bed throw is from Denis Colomb.** FOLLOWING SPREAD: **The tree, which was cleaned up and pruned to reveal its shape, serves as a shelter for outdoor dining. The table is by Mario Bellini.**

CLARE GRAHAM
AND BOB BREEN'S
MORYORK
HIGHLAND PARK

Who would expect such a dizzying haul of found objects and sculpture behind the unassuming facade of a commercial building in the middle of Highland Park? In the early twentieth century, this neighborhood and next-door Pasadena became havens for artists and architects who were disciples of the Arts and Crafts movement. Unfortunately, it later became known for gang violence. However, when a small supermarket came up for sale in 1986, the artist and collector Clare Graham and his partner, Bob Breen, bought it as a studio space for Graham. Since then, Highland Park has been transformed into an up-and-coming neighborhood that still has a lot of Arts and Crafts houses dating back to the early twentieth century, although sadly many were demolished in the mid-1950s. Graham and Breen named the studio MorYork, and today Graham opens the building occasionally for art exhibitions and events.

Over time, Graham has created an extraordinary space, which is layered with his sculpture and raw materials, including probably everything ever manufactured that could be bought in a store—bottle caps, buttons, colanders, dominoes, Scrabble tiles, old teeth (yes, old teeth), and even false eyes. He has built a career on making art with recycled materials, and his studio is filled to the brim with sculptures that defy the imagination. Some resemble functional furniture, like a wire-covered armoire decorated with round, flat metal plates, or a stool covered in ring-top pulls. However, the predominant objects have an otherworldly quality, made from mounds of colored beads or soda cans.

OPPOSITE: The stairs lead up to the guest bedroom. Underneath is a collection of pale green pottery and a Herman Miller Zenith armchair in seafoam green. PAGE 132: Under the stairs, a knot-wood table holds a collection of ivory, a mercury-glass sphere, and a Dirk van Erp lamp with a mica shade. PAGE 133: Hanging in the stairwell is a twisted copper wire sculpture by D'Lisa Creager.

OPPOSITE: In the kitchen, orange California Fiestaware enlivens the gray cupboards. A white art deco glass pendant light hangs from the ceiling. ABOVE: The dining table is surrounded by a set of vintage Robert Mallet-Stevens metal chairs. Sculptural pieces by Graham include a hanging sculpture and wrapped balls in an open metal bookcase.

Which is why it comes as a surprise to discover that their newly built house, conveniently located on what was once the supermarket parking lot behind MorYork, is sparsely furnished. Graham and Breen hired architect Robert Kerr to design a house that still had the feeling of a studio, with industrial-style high beamed ceilings and concrete walls, plus space for a houseguest or two.

The entrance is inconspicuous, with a short walkway leading to a yellow door—a rare note of color in this monochromatic two-story building. Inside, all views lead to a central open garden courtyard; most of the windows at this level slide away to create an indoor-outdoor space that extends the house. The main bedroom is tucked away under a mezzanine guest quarters, with just a few shuttered windows keeping the room peacefully dark. Graham's collection of found paintings hung here are flea market treasures, including a pair of

Tony Duquette framed maquettes found in a monthly Pasadena market.

Past a well-ordered kitchen, the floor level drops down to accommodate a studio-like space, dominated by a large abstract expressionist painting by Shay Rieger from 1954. Here, Graham has hung several of his own works, including a large, hanging, plaited phone wire art piece. However, it seems only a matter of time before more of the phantasmagoric pieces from next door will elbow their way in.

OPPOSITE, LEFT: A plaited phone wire sculpture by Graham helps define the kitchen from the living space. OPPOSITE, RIGHT: A vast sixty-inch-diameter concave lens in a corner of Graham's studio reflects the surrounding sculptures, which are also by him. Hanging from the ceiling is a *Cloud* sculpture by Blanka Šperková along with another Graham piece—a suspended mass of aluminum pop-tops. ABOVE, LEFT: An ornate cabinet with an embroidered surface of titanium beads, silver leaf, and concave and convex mirrors by Graham takes center stage in the studio. ABOVE, RIGHT: A titanium beaded wire sculpture by Graham.

PART II
LOS ANGELES MODERN

Some of the most groundbreaking examples of mid-century residential modernism can be found in Los Angeles, thanks to a wide variety of influential architects experimenting with materials and structure. Many of these houses are being renovated and sensitively reworked for today's needs.

OPPOSITE: Inspired by the English Punch and Judy puppet show, Peter Shire dressed up his TV set to capture the experience.

ADAM BLACKMAN'S
J. R. STEIN HOUSE
BY A. QUINCY JONES
CRESTWOOD HILLS

If you are searching for the hard to find, the eclectic, the unusual, and at times even shocking furniture, lighting, and decorative objects spanning centuries of design, the mid-Hollywood furniture store Blackman Cruz has long been the place to go. Since 1993, David Cruz and Adam Blackman have combined their very different aesthetics to make the kind of emporium that decorators from all over the world consider a must-see.

So, when Blackman and his wife, Kate, went house hunting, they were not looking for just any old house. It was a stroke of luck to find a relatively untouched A. Quincy Jones house in Crestwood Hills, a hillside suburb of Brentwood. Designed in the late 1940s as low-income housing for 500, only 160 of the homes were built, and between a Bel Air fire and obsessive redevelopment, very few original A. Quincy Jones houses have survived.

When Jones opened his first studio in 1945, he welcomed the chance to contribute to John Entenza's formative Case Study House program and worked tirelessly throughout his life on university and office buildings. However, his main enthusiasm was for low-income housing integrated into suburban greenbelts. He transformed simple tract houses into small but creatively designed homes using walls of glass, high ceilings, and post-and-beam construction.

This three-bedroom house needed a lot of restoration; Blackman brought in Rick Cortez of RAC Design Build to help strip the structure back and rebuild it. There was a lot of work ahead as the walls and ceilings had

OPPOSITE: A Chinese root chair sits against the restored paneled wall next to a Venetian mirror. The blue art glass vase was bought in London. FOLLOWING SPREAD: The main sitting room sofas by William "Billy" Haines sit opposite a blue painting over the fireplace by Eric Orr. The house is designated a Los Angeles Historic-Cultural Monument.

OPPOSITE: The dining room table and Gazelle chairs are by Dan Johnson; a Miracle chandelier by Bakalowits & Söhne hangs above. ABOVE: The rare leather 1968 Seagull chair was designed by Gösta Berg and Sten Erik Eriksson for Fritz Hansen. The walnut sideboard is by George Nakashima.

been painted white, and Jones's ingenuously designed louvered panels were nailed shut. Somehow a guesthouse was attached to the house, which was a squeeze on such a small parcel of land, and the bathrooms and kitchen needed a lot of renovating. It took months and much patience to strip and sandblast the walls—but the result was transformative.

Blackman reconfigured the entry, giving it a small, landscaped court-yard that can now be seen through the redesigned galley kitchen window. With the help of the architects, he extended the dining room, designing it around his collection of rare Don Johnson Gazelle chairs and a matching table. The small sitting room replaced an unused patio, while the guesthouse was reworked into a guest room and study. The next priority was to provide

ABOVE: This cabinet features relics from past buying trips, including a Jacques Lipchitz sketch, unsigned bronze abstracts, a German nineteenth-century monkey nodder, Black Forest–carved wooden crocodiles, and random pieces that eventually make their way to the Blackman Cruz store. OPPOSITE: The kitchen was carefully restored. Above the sink hang Chinese yokes from the 1900s used for carrying water.

space for a lifetime of collecting, adding sympathetically designed built-in cupboards and shelving. Since the house was built with simple, affordable materials, such as Douglas fir, redwood, concrete block, and glass, Blackman continued his additions in the same vein, recycling old doors and recreating original cabinet pull knobs.

Conveniently, a long built-in wardrobe remained in the main bedroom, but now one of the windows has a view of the nearby Getty Center on the other side of the canyon. Steps lead down to the main living room, where shelves hold a treasure trove of Blackman's collections. Anchored by a matching pair of William "Billy" Haines sofas, this room includes Blackman's library of reference books, art and sculpture, and a cozy fireplace. The couple are always on alert for the next wildfire to sweep Crestwood Hills, but wouldn't choose to live anywhere else.

ABOVE AND OPPOSITE: The bed in the main bedroom was custom-built by Rick Cortez; the bedside tables are by Ico Parisi.

MARY WEATHERFORD'S
PILOT HOUSE
BY A. QUINCY JONES AND WHITNEY R. SMITH
LA'S EASTSIDE

L os Angeles artist Mary Weatherford is known for her large abstract paintings on linen that often include illuminated lighting tubes. While her work appears vividly unrestrained, she is a meticulous artist, and her renovation of the Pilot House by mid-century modern architect A. Quincy Jones reflects this. The landmark building is just over 1,500 square feet and sits on a hillside looking rather like a long tramcar, with a dramatically angular roof. Called the Pilot House because it was originally a showhouse for Jones and his partner, Whitney R. Smith, it was built in 1948 as a continuation of their experiment with well-designed low-cost housing and was to be part of an unrealized

**DECORATED BY
OLIVER M. FURTH**

affordable development on the hillsides overlooking LA's Eastside.

Weatherford bought the house over seven years ago and lived in it for about a year to see how it functioned. Concerned about getting the renovation right, she brought in a team of designers and restorers. She hired the firm Escher GuneWardena to help restore the structure, which involved stripping the white-painted ceilings and walls and turning a back porch into a library without changing the building's footprint. The work took four years and included installing a new roof and air-conditioning as well as combining two small bedrooms into one.

Fortunately, a relic of the original, green-stained wood was discovered inside a drawer, which provided a handy guide for colorist Scott

OPPOSITE: A view of a sculptural wooden stool, with the kitchen in the background. FOLLOWING SPREAD: The 1948 Pilot House, designed by A. Quincy Jones and Whitney R. Smith, has landscaping by Native Sanctuary and Tivoli Landscape Design. This extensively restored house has been designated a Los Angeles Historic-Cultural Monument.

RIGHT: In the living room, Hans Wegner lounge chairs sit opposite custom sofas. The side table is by Piet Hein Eek.
FOLLOWING SPREAD: The Saarinen dining table by Knoll is surrounded by Niels Otto Møller rosewood chairs.

Flax, who restored the newly stripped plywood to its original look. As an artist who works with color, Weatherford fully realized this was an important step as much of the house, both inside and out, was constructed with this material.

Decorator Oliver M. Furth stepped in, working hand in glove with Weatherford to help with the house's furnishings. This was a special project for Furth, who has long been associated with the decorative arts; he is known as a chair emeritus of the Decorative Arts and Design Council of the Los Angeles County Museum of Art. As the house was once designed for low-income owners, much of the furniture was originally built-in, and Weatherford tried to replicate this. During the research on the house, she and Furth found original drawings for the sofa, which they had recreated. Much of the other furniture came from collections Weatherford had accumulated over the years, which included mid-century classics as well as more contemporary pieces from Los Angeles designers that Furth helped edit down.

ABOVE AND OPPOSITE: **In the kitchen, the original plywood color is now revealed, after being stripped back and restored by colorist Scott Flax.**

Up a steep hillside, steps lead to a generous back terrace. This was intended to give an impression of spaciousness to the small house, also pushing it further into the view. The windows run along the whole front of the house, and clerestory windows open to cool the building in hot weather. A pair of Hans Wegner armchairs faces the new sofa, backed by a freestanding orange fireplace, which sits on a large, flat stone slab. The furnishings carry on the natural materials and textures of the house, drawn from European mid-century classic designers like Charles Stendig, Poul Kjærholm, and Grete Jalk.

Weatherford exhibits in galleries around the world, and when she returns to Los Angeles she especially enjoys the warm and welcoming main bedroom with its orange furnishings punctuated by a Serge Mouille wall light, and the peace of the hillside around her.

OPPOSITE: On a wall above the bed in the main bedroom is a Serge Mouille sconce. The table lamp is by Greta Magnusson Grossman. ABOVE: A Noguchi lamp is handily placed next to a leather sofa by Poul Kjærholm in the same room. FOLLOWING SPREAD: A set of Hay Palissade outdoor dining chairs sits around a dining table on the back patio.

ELLEN DEGENERES AND PORTIA DE ROSSI'S
BRODY HOUSE
BY A. QUINCY JONES
HOLMBY HILLS

Characteristically, almost all of the houses owned by Ellen DeGeneres and Portia de Rossi have been both dramatic and architecturally significant, and none more so than this mid-century modern masterpiece, designed in the late 1940s by the iconic Los Angeles architect A. Quincy Jones, with interiors by the legendary Hollywood decorator William "Billy" Haines. Commissioned by society couple and collectors Frances and Sidney Brody, it was once home to a vast ceramic mural by Matisse in its outdoor enclosed courtyard, and a museum-quality collection of contemporary paintings, including work by Picasso and Braque.

**DECORATED BY
JANE HALLWORTH**

DeGeneres bought the house several years ago, bringing in designer Jane Hallworth, who furnished it with a considerable amount of William "Billy" Haines furniture, especially in the large, enclosed patio, which opens up through French doors. Here, the outdoor fireplace and original waterfall fountain wall have been restored, but sadly the famous Matisse mural was donated to the Los Angeles County Museum of Art well before the show-business couple bought the 11,000-square-foot house.

Throughout the property you can see endless repetitions of the indoor-outdoor theme. Dining room shelving appears to flow through a glass window to hover over an

OPPOSITE: **The Brody House entry passage includes a bench by Claude Lalanne and a hanging wire sculpture by Ruth Asawa.**

ornamental pool, and glass doors slide back to create an open-to-the-elements space. Along the entry passage reaching up to the next floor is a unique "floating" staircase. With angular shapes, it looks like a piece of sculpture fixed to the wall.

DeGeneres's taste includes a medley of 1940s French furniture designers from about the same period as the house: Jacques Adnet, Jean Prouvé, and Charlotte Perriand, all of whom were pioneers of French modernism. Hallworth says that they bought about 80 percent of the furniture specifically for this house, deciding also to collect Danish and French

ABOVE: The entry's front doors have their original hardware. Here, the indoor-outdoor design of the house is first revealed. OPPOSITE: In the entry passage, the stairs lead up to the bedrooms and other private areas of the house. At left, underneath the staircase, a mirror wall was replaced with a large collaborative painting by Jean-Michel Basquiat and Andy Warhol titled *Hot Water*, 1985 (© *Estate of Jean-Michel Basquiat. Licensed by Artestar, New York /* © 2023 The Andy Warhol Foundation for the Visual Arts, Inc. / Licensed by Artists Rights Society (ARS), New York). The daybed is by Jean Prouvé.

mid-century pieces and contemporary artists' work that would sit well with the Prouvé and Perriand furniture. It became an inventive mix of masters: Jean Royère, Pierre Jeanneret, Mogens Koch, Poul Kjærholm, and Frits Henningsen with the likes of Mats Theselius, Michael Wilson, and Rick Owens for good measure. Today, the harmonious furnishings look like they completely belong within the house's elegant abstract walls.

DeGeneres and de Rossi were determined to restore a lot of the original details. Hallworth and de Rossi worked side by side on-site for the duration of the renovation, bringing the palette back to the original, although they weren't afraid to add new, modern touches. The Rick Owens long, chunky dining table is contemporary, and parallels a custom cabinet designed by Hallworth. She furnished the living room that looks out to the central courtyard using DeGeneres's favorite monochrome palette, adding custom sofas around a mid-century wooden-slatted coffee table. A small round games table sits in one corner, surrounded by mid-century modern French chairs by Jeanneret.

The kitchen was updated with Gaggenau appliances, stainless-steel and marble countertops, and lower cabinets of stained walnut. Upstairs, several rooms were converted into a single suite encompassing Haines's original cork shelving into a sitting room and library off the main bedroom. The light fittings were designed to stylistically pull the furnishings together. When they were installed, the fixtures were dynamic and architectural and felt as if they had always been part of the fabric of the house. The pièce de résistance was Oscar Niemeyer's enormous, glowing sun fixture in the media room, which made the celestial-based narrative Haines initiated seem complete.

OPPOSITE: In the dining area, a Mies van der Rohe leather daybed has a view of the garden. ABOVE: Here, glass walls enclose the house, filling it with light and providing unobstructed garden views. A. Quincy Jones designed the building to move seamlessly indoors and outdoors. PAGE 170: Above the fireplace hangs a rare ceiling fixture by Oscar Niemeyer; opposite the sofa is an original Arne Jacobsen Egg chair and ottoman. The coffee table is a mid-century carpenters table from Blackman Cruz. PAGE 171: A table by Rick Owens commands the dining room; the chairs are by Jean Prouvé and the chandelier is by Jean Royère.

ABOVE: An original William "Billy" Haines built-in desk is a standout in a guest bedroom. OPPOSITE: In an extension of the living room, a second dining area has a set of armchairs by Pierre Jeanneret that surround a PK54 table by Poul Kjærholm. Above hangs a William Haines chandelier, original to the house.

ABOVE: On the main bedroom hearth sits a mid-century American ceramic lamp. OPPOSITE: In the bedroom, an original William Haines built-in shelf holds a nineteenth-century wood staircase maquette. On the wall hangs a collection of anonymous mid-century oil paintings.

CRAIG ELLWOOD'S 1956 HOUSE

MALIBU

More than just a strip of houses along a beachfront, the town of Malibu spreads up to the hills overlooking the coast with an eclectic mix of housing, mostly with a scenic view of the ocean. Decorator and design writer Mallery Roberts Morgan was brought in to help when her clients bought a house here by the well-

DECORATED BY MALLERY ROBERTS MORGAN

known mid-century modern architect Craig Ellwood. This residence was built in 1956 for a school principal who admired the simplicity of Ellwood's Case Study Houses, which were part of a group of houses commissioned by *Arts & Architecture* magazine between the 1940s and the 1960s to showcase affordable new houses built with innovative techniques and inexpensive materials.

Since the house was previously well re-stored by an earlier owner, Roberts Morgan could focus on furnishings to suit her European clients; they wanted a comfortable setting that retained the mid-century modern vibe, as well as personalizing it for their cosmopolitan lifestyle. Roberts Morgan restored the original carpeting throughout, drawing from a vintage photograph of the house. This linked the rooms and eased the cold rectangular grid of the floors; she also added creamy cotton floor-to-ceiling curtains that softened the harsh modernism of the steel and glass windows. The redwood paneling in the sitting room is original to the house.

Roberts Morgan kept to the architectural style by adding mid-century modern furniture, as well as a very comfortable sofa from Flexform. The house has its own rectangular grid, which gives it a certain dynamism, and the windows all around open wide, providing the feeling of an

OPPOSITE: A painting by the architect Craig Ellwood overlooks the dining table. The pendant light is by Gino Sarfatti.

ABOVE: In the entryway hangs a painting by Tadaaki Kuwayama, *Untitled*, 1962. A ceramic vase, by LA-based artist Caroline Blackburn, holds philodendron leaves from the garden.
OPPOSITE: The furniture in the living room includes chairs by Charles and Ray Eames and Pierre Paulin. A painting by Armando Marroco hangs above the fireplace. A colorful small Eames storage unit sits against the wall; the coffee table is by Paolo Piva.

open pavilion. The kitchen, with its original mahogany-veneered cabinets and laminate counters, opens onto a dining space where her clients hung a painting by Craig Ellwood "on the diagonal" as instructed on the back.

To increase the size of this modestly designed two-bedroom house, Robert Morgan also furnished the outdoor living spaces—adding a large scrim to shelter a back courtyard that forms an outdoor dining room conveniently next to the kitchen, where large groups of friends can gather. The poolside deck and gazebo have as much floor space as the house—enough to accommodate another set of outdoor upholstered seating, as well as a dining table under the pool house rafters. Here, at the edge of the garden, the view of the Pacific Ocean takes center stage.

OPPOSITE, LEFT: An armchair and stool by Bruno Mathsson sits in front of an artwork by John Giorno. OPPOSITE, RIGHT: A photograph of Capri by Francesco Jodice (© Francesco Jodice) hangs in an interior hallway. ABOVE: The extended courtyard, reworked by Roberts Morgan with Terremoto Landscape Architects, adds to the dining spaces of the house. The custom table centers the outdoor area and is surrounded by Walter Lamb chairs. FOLLOWING SPREAD: The long, low exterior is typical of Craig Ellwood's acclaimed mid-century residential buildings.

MARK HADDAWY'S
HARPEL HOUSE
BY JOHN LAUTNER
HOLLYWOOD HILLS

By the time veteran house restorer and designer Mark Haddawy came across this Hollywood Hills house by John Lautner, a second story had been added onto the roof, as well as track lighting, extra stucco walls, and aluminum windows. Very few conservators had the knowledge or the right tradesmen to take it back to the original 1956 design. However, after three years of Haddawy's restoration, the once elegant house began to emerge. Radio announcer Willis Harpel commissioned the house, as well as a small circular studio below the building that was never built. By following the original plans, Haddawy is now constructing it for the first time, making modifications to comply with today's building codes.

The property is reached via a steep driveway. In the garden, Lautner began a gazebo-like interplay of beams around a central column that he continued as a structural idea into the house. Upon entry, the eye is drawn to the even larger column that appears to support the entire roof of the house with its radiating beams—including an octagonal skylight that Haddawy rebuilt according to the original drawings. These also provided the blueprint for Lautner's built-in furniture, which Haddaway also reconstructed: a built-in sofa, bookshelves, and the kitchen cabinets and cooking island. The living room is sunken to provide a higher ceiling and a change of level in this essentially one-story house. Lautner characteristically used natural materials to soften his fundamentally geometric structures—the fireplace is defined by a large concrete slab set into a rock wall, with wooden beams overhead.

OPPOSITE: Glass walls hang like clear screens from the post-and-beam Harpel House and provide exterior/interior views. This extensively restored house is designated a Los Angeles Historic-Cultural Monument. FOLLOWING SPREAD: The structure of the house flows from the outdoor beams into the interior.

The front of the house and the swimming pool are oriented to take advantage of the distant views, which reach out across the San Fernando Valley. Haddawy's home showcases his extensive collection of pre-Columbian pottery and masks, as well as French furniture from about the same period as the house, including designers Jean Prouvé and Charlotte Perriand.

PREVIOUS SPREAD: A collection of books, along with a Picasso vase and small pre-Columbian sculptures, have been placed on the reconstructed sitting room bookcase. Stools in front of the rebuilt sofa are by Charlotte Perriand. A black marble Louise Bourgeois 1968 sculpture sits on the dining table. ABOVE: The swimming pool has extensive views over the San Fernando Valley to the San Gabriel Mountains.

GARCIA HOUSE

BY JOHN LAUTNER
HOLLYWOOD HILLS

When Hollywood insiders John McIlwee and Bill Damaschke decided to go house hunting, they had no intention of buying this unrestored mid-century modern house that hung dangerously over a Los Angeles canyon. However, they decided to take a big leap into the unknown because the Garcia House, one of the most dramatic houses built by architect John Lautner in the early 1960s, had a lot of potential despite needing a substantial amount of work.

Here, Lautner continued his exploration of unconventional house shapes; a year earlier he had just finished the Chemisphere House, known as the "flying saucer house" because it looked as though it had just landed from outer space in the Hollywood Hills. The Garcia House is just as striking in its own way, with its almond-shaped hillside facade, although it

has a more conventional central outdoor curved staircase, it still challenges expectations of what a home should look like. It was built for Russell Garcia, a film composer and conductor and his wife, Gina Garcia, who briefly lived in it before they set sail around the world.

McIlwee and Damaschke lived there for a while in order to understand it. After a lot of research, they hired the architectural firm Marmol Radziner, who had handled many high-profile projects, including mid-century modern residential classics by Richard Neutra and Albert Frey, and they brought this mid-century masterpiece back to its original light-filled condition.

Overlooking a canyon above Sunset Boulevard through big, colored-glass, thirty-foot-tall windows, the house looks bigger than it really is—spanning about 2,700 square feet on just over an acre of sloping land. Split into two parts, the main living space occupies half of the curved building on one side, while two

OPPOSITE: The original exterior stairway curves down to the main rooms of the Garcia House from the street. FOLLOWING SPREAD: The house is also called the Rainbow House, thanks to its multicolored windows; the Lautner-designed pool was added in 2008.

RIGHT: Saporiti club chairs, ottomans, and a sofa surround a custom Lucite coffee table in the living room.

bedrooms and a study fill the other half, divided by the central outdoor staircase.

The house was decorated by Darren Brown, who later helped with the couple's 1970s Gerald and Betty Ford house in Rancho Mirage. Brown looked to the same period for the Garcia House—here, front and center in the dining area is a set of 1974 Saporiti dining chairs surrounding a Brown-designed dining table. Stepping down into the main living room, a built-in bookcase by the architects floats above a long, and curved sofa, also from Saporiti, the large

ABOVE: The original stone fireplace in the living room is designed to fit into the curve of the roof. OPPOSITE: In the living room, the coffee table is by Charles Hollis Jones; the curved Arco floor lamp is by Achille and Pier Giacomo Castiglioni for Flos. Architects Marmol Radziner designed the stained walnut cabinetry. The photographic portrait is by Terry Richardson.

room dazzles with its window panels of colored glass. A lush, comfortable, thick carpet softens the hard modernist edges of the space.

The original plans for the house included a swimming pool, which was unbuilt, but planned to echo the shape of the house exterior. To add it was a design challenge, as building codes have dramatically changed in the Hollywood Hills since the 1960s, mainly because of earthquakes. Today, it adds a dramatic finishing touch to this historic property.

OPPOSITE: The dining room table was designed by Darren Brown, the chandelier is original to the house, and the dining chairs are 1974 Saporiti. ABOVE: A copper pendant lamp hangs next to the guest bedroom. The Cityscape bedside tables are by Paul Evans. FOLLOWING SPREAD: In the main bedroom, a Venini lamp sits on a custom table by Darren Brown. Diane Arbus photographs are displayed next to the Lucite four-poster bed by Charles Hollis Jones. Above the bed hangs a painting by Kirsten Everberg. The rug is an Ebbtide carpet, designed by Edward Fields in 1960.

SILVERTOP
BY JOHN LAUTNER
SILVER LAKE

One of the most difficult moments in an architect's career is coming to terms with a house they have spent years designing that has been left unfinished due to lack of money. In 1958, architect John Lautner was very unhappy when work stopped on Silvertop, one of his most adventurous houses on top of a hill overlooking Silver Lake. Here, he had incorporated many avant-garde ideas, such as remote-controlled wood louver glass panels in the bedroom and an entire front glass wall that slid away, not to mention installing what may be the world's first infinity pool in the 1950s.

RESTORED BY BARBARA BESTOR WITH DECORATOR JAMIE BUSH

The house was sadly left abandoned for many years, then briefly owned by a couple who struggled with the maintenance costs, although the home did make a brief appearance in the 1987 film *Less Than Zero*, based on the novel of the same name by Bret Easton Ellis.

It took the new owner, Luke Wood, who bought the rundown property over fifty years later, to finish Lautner's dream house. Wood brought in the team of decorator Jamie Bush and architect Barbara Bestor of Bestor Architects to restore the house, including revamping its hidden mechanisms. They worked on the project for over three years, immeasurably aided by Lautner's original plans, safely stored away at the J. Paul Getty Museum. Today's technological advances upgraded the house: new digital and updated motorized systems meant that there was no need to intrusively dig through walls while LED fixtures and contemporary sound systems were hidden behind new cork ceiling panels sourced from Portugal.

OPPOSITE: A view of downtown Los Angeles through the rebuilt Silvertop pivoting glass door.
FOLLOWING SPREAD: The living room overview shows the curved concrete fireplace with its plaster finish. Jamie Bush designed much of the furniture except for the green chairs by Arne Norell and the Jens Risom white chair on the right-hand side of the fireplace.

RIGHT: The dining area is filled with a curved built-in bench and a floor lamp, both designed by Bush; and the rounded table is from the Egg Collective in New York.

ABOVE: The new kitchen has been redesigned with vertical bands of thin cypress slats; it is lit from above by square-shaped skylights. OPPOSITE, LEFT: The new kitchen sink and stainless-steel appliances were brought in by Ilan Dei Studio. The ceiling throughout is made of cork. OPPOSITE, RIGHT: The kitchen banquette, designed by Bush, was integrated into the space with cypress slats.

A long, curving driveway steeply ascends to the house, where the original cast-bronze front door leads inside. A curved concrete roof soars like a large seashell over the main living space, while the front glass wall slides away to open the room up to a broad outdoor terrace overlooking Silver Lake and the towering skyscrapers in the distance of downtown Los Angeles. Centered by a curving concrete fireplace, this space feels bigger than it looks as there are no intrusive columns to break up the room, although it presents a decorating challenge since seating areas had to become free-form in this rounded space.

Bush custom-designed much of the furniture, including a double-sided sofa, and a round rug in the sitting room to echo the curved fireplace. Custom cypress cabinetry hides the television and audio equipment. The kitchen was remade with fluted cypress paneling and subtly modernized. Bestor Architects added a breakfast corner and banquette and

gave the utilitarian space a new kitchen island. A sliding brick panel above the kitchen counter opens upward rather than across for access to the living area.

Bush carefully balanced appropriateness with comfort since this architectural masterpiece had to function as a family home for the owners and their two children. Pillows, cushions, faux-fur throws, and plenty of rugs make this austere concrete house warm and welcoming.

OPPOSITE: The main bedroom has a concrete fireplace with a large boulder embedded within its facade. The ceiling can retract to reveal a skylight, while the slat wood windows close to become a solid wall. ABOVE: The new indoor-outdoor bathroom has retracting glass walls and ceiling. FOLLOWING SPREAD: The house has been extensively restored by architect Barbara Bestor, who upgraded the opening panoramic windows using current technology. PAGES 216–217: At this level, brick and wood walls curve around the house exterior. The tower, part of the original design, was never built. It has been added by the new owners.

GIAMPIERO TAGLIAFERRI

SILVER LAKE

The hip urban district of Silver Lake sits on the east side of East Hollywood, and thanks to its relatively remote distance from LA's Westside, has always attracted outlaws and rebels. It is said that there are more architecturally significant houses, including some designed by the most celebrated architects of the mid-century modern movement, here than in any other part of the city.

You will find buildings by Gregory Ain, Craig Ellwood, and John Lautner, as well as Richard Neutra's home and studio, which was named a National Historic Landmark in 2017. Austrian-born architect Rudolph Schindler designed several houses and apartment buildings in the area, and, in 1939, his colleague Edward Richard Lind built this small house nearby, with views across the Silver Lake Reservoir.

The home's proportions, views, and easy open style attracted Italian designer Giampiero Tagliaferri when he was sent to Los Angeles seven years ago to oversee the design of the Oliver Peoples eyeglass stores. The house was in good shape: since its Japanese-like proportions and wood-paneled walls had been maintained, Tagliaferri's main challenge was to furnish it with his very personal collection of twentieth-century furniture. He also decided to take a step back from Oliver Peoples (although he still works for the company as a consultant) and become a full-fledged designer.

The open-plan ground floor has two interior wings, creating space for two sitting rooms, centered by a dining area in the middle. Leading directly from the entry, the first seating area is furnished with a Civingam sofa by De Pas, D'Urbino, Lomazzi, and an

OPPOSITE: A view of the corner of the living room features a Ricardo Fasanello Anel chair.
FOLLOWING SPREAD: Tagliaferri furnished a section of the main room with Oscar Niemeyer's Alta chair and ottoman; a Jonathan De Pas, Donato D'Urbino, and Paolo Lomazzi Civingam sofa; and a Jean Claude Dresse coffee table, all from the 1970s. The Franca Stagi and Cesare Leonardi Ribbon CL9 chair is from the 1960s; the side table is by Osvaldo Borsani. A 1968 etched screen print by Lucio Fontana hangs above the fireplace.

RIGHT: The living room includes a Joe Colombo white leather Elda chair, Luigi Colani's Orbis modular sofa, Gae Aulenti's Jumbo coffee table, and a pair of Ricardo Fasanello Anel chairs, found on 1stDibs. The print at the right is by John Baldessari.

RIGHT: In the dining area, a Gianni Celada pendant light for Fontana Arte hangs above a vintage Italian marble table, surrounded by George Nelson swag-leg chairs.

Alta chair and ottoman by Oscar Niemeyer found on the furniture website 1stDibs. A fiberglass Ribbon chair by Cesare Leonardi and Franca Stagi from 1961 finishes the room arrangement like a piece of sculpture.

The second seating area has a different feel, notable for the large off-white leather Elda chair by Italian designer Joe Colombo. Inspired by a visit to a shipyard in 1963, he named it after his wife. Tagliaferri chose open circular chairs by Ricardo Fasanello so as not to block the remark-able view across the valley to the Franklin Hills. In a nod to the original wooden walls throughout the house, the seating area is overlooked by a large Senufo African bird sculpture. Next to the kitchen in the dining room, Tagliaferri hung a Fonda Arte pendant light over a vintage Italian marble dining table surrounded with George Nelson swag-leg chairs. Along one side of the space, an original built-in cabinet functions as a storage area

and a serving table. Here, Tagliaferri added piles of books and a table lamp by Ettore Sottsass.

Stairs lead up to the second floor where Tagliaferri chose to sleep in the smaller bedroom with the best views rather than the larger one downstairs. Set in a paneled niche, the bed is flanked by a pair of sconces by Carlo Nason for Mazzega. Currently, he has far-flung design projects, from Los Angeles to Milan, where he applies his expert eye to color, design, and furniture—specializing in twentieth-century Italian and California modernism.

OPPOSITE: The kitchen is accented with an Eric Roinestad vase, an Angelo Mangiarotti table lamp, a Jonathan Cross bowl, and a photograph by Herb Ritts. The ceiling fixture is original to the house. ABOVE: Paolo Piva's 1980s Adia daybed anchors one end of the sunny terrace. It is joined by Emma Gismondi Schweinberger's Tondara table and Magistretti Vicario armchairs.

FIROOZ ZAHEDI'S WILSHIRE TERRACE APARTMENT

BY VICTOR GRUEN
LITTLE HOLMBY

Westwood is the home of the famed University of California, Los Angeles (UCLA), and Westwood Boulevard, its main thoroughfare, is lined with condominium towers. Some have a strong architectural presence, and photographer Firooz Zahedi's building on this street, which continues into adjacent Little Holmby, is no exception. Designed by prominent mid-century modern architect Victor Gruen in 1958, the building comes complete with an elegant glass-filled lobby and a porte cochere. Zahedi and his wife, the well-known collector Beth Rudin DeWoody, have gradually accumulated three apartments in this building—without a doubt attracted to its central location and the arcadian northern views over the palm tree–filled Westside hills.

While each apartment contains an extraordinary amount of art, this set of rooms is devoted to Zahedi's archives and personal collections that reflect his close ties with Andy Warhol, who first employed him as a photographer, as well as the legendary Elizabeth Taylor, who became a close friend. It took around four to five months to renovate and rework the space, taking out a wet bar, refacing the fireplace with travertine marble, and adding art lighting. Zahedi upgraded the kitchen countertops and designed the linoleum floor to keep to the 1950s vibe. Finally, he painted the walls with a calm, pale gray, a perfect background to showcase his art and photography collections.

OPPOSITE: An Andy Warhol silk screen portrait, *Marilyn Monroe (Marilyn)*, 1967 (© 2023 The Andy Warhol Foundation for the Visual Arts, Inc. / Licensed by Artists Rights Society (ARS), New York), gifted to Firooz Zahedi by Warhol, hangs above a Lucite table.

ABOVE: A coffee table found in Palm Springs sits in front of a sitting room sofa furnished with pieces from Zahedi's textile collection. opposite: In the bedroom, Zahedi had the dramatic built-in bedhead stained and refinished by Jim Goodrich. The bedspread is vintage Moroccan. An artwork by Edward Kienholz hangs above the bed. FOLLOWING SPREAD: On the dining table amid many books on photography are a pair of vintage candelabra from the Beverly Hills Hilton. The skateboards on the wall are redone with *Khatamkari*, a marquetry pattern with pieces of wood by Leila Nazarian.In the far left corner are vintage film reels combined with sculptures by Yassi Mazandi placed in front of a Frank Stella lithograph titled *Star of Persia*.

SAVILE ROW AND AMERICA

STEVEN AND WILLIAM LADD : MARY QUEEN OF THE UNIVERSE

NG LUCKY   LUCIEN PELLAT-FINET

APERTURE PAUL STRAND NATIONAL GALLERY OF ART

ART KANE

Robert & Ethel Scull: Portrait of a Collection   GOLDMAN

JO ANN CALLIS

Fortune   FEBRUARY 19

Fortune   NOVEMBER 1947

BACKYARD OASIS   THE SWIMMING POOL IN SOUTHERN
CALIFORNIA PHOTOGRAPHY

HOLLYWOOD   FIROOZ ZAHEDI

HOLLYWOOD   FIROOZ ZAHEDI

HOLLYWOOD   FIROOZ ZAHEDI

The Legend   Serpent King

OZ

LEONARD FREED

IN PRISON HALL

THE NEW YORK SCHOOL
PHOTOGRAPHS 1936-1963

THE WELL LOOK

Furnishing the apartment wasn't much of a problem as Zahedi has owned various homes in Los Angeles over the years and has accumulated an impressive collection of twentieth-century furniture. In the main living space, there are side tables by Paul Frankl and a coffee table that was found in Palm Springs. The dramatic brown brutalist combined bedhead and side tables were a secondhand furniture shop discovery that Zahedi had stained black by Jim Goodrich of Cache Antiques. Zahedi also had furniture custom-made or altered to suit his particular vision. Nods to his Iranian heritage appear on a Persian table in the entry and in various artworks in the apartment, including a pair of skateboards redone with *Khatamkari* marquetry patterns with pieces of wood by Leila Nazarian.

OPPOSITE, RIGHT: A photo by Ed Ruscha of the exterior of Zahedi's 1958 Victor Gruen building leans against a bookcase. ABOVE: In the entry, a collection of eclectic objects, artworks, and photographs sits atop a Florence Knoll sideboard.

Hardly a wall remains uncovered by art or sculpture, some by Zahedi himself and others by friends like Yassi Mazandi, as well as a museum-quality photo collection that includes works by Baron Adolph de Meyer, Dennis Hopper, Irving Penn, André Kertész, and Helmut Newton. Books are everywhere, on almost every surface, especially because in recent years Zahedi has produced several volumes of his own work and is the photographer of two other publications. The most recent is *Look at Me*, a collection of Zahedi's photos documenting Hollywood's biggest stars for magazines like *Vanity Fair*, and studio movie posters, while *My Elizabeth* is a visual reflection of his thirty-five-year friendship with Elizabeth Taylor.

ABOVE: The streamlined kitchen is mainly original to the mid-century modern style, circa 1958. Zahedi designed the new floor, replaced the countertop with Caesarstone, and added new appliances. OPPOSITE: A Color Field artwork by Gene Davis hangs on the fireplace that Zahedi resurfaced with travertine marble.

SIR ELTON JOHN AND DAVID FURNISH'S
SIERRA TOWERS APARTMENT

BY JACK A. CHARNAY
BEVERLY HILLS

When Sir Elton John and his spouse, film producer David Furnish, needed a West Coast apartment, they turned to a friend, the Los Angeles–based British decorator Martyn Lawrence Bullard, to help find them a convenient location. The apartment they found in the iconic Sierra Towers building has jaw-dropping vistas of snowy topped mountains, and Los Angeles spreads out like a map below. The building was constructed in 1965, which proved to be an important starting point for the project as Bullard and Furnish decided to look to the 1960s and

**DECORATED BY
MARTYN LAWRENCE
BULLARD**

1970s for the furnishings, and to draw on the couple's huge collections for the art.

Even though this apartment is over 3,000 square feet, the real work was to convert its cramped spaces. Walls were taken down, bedrooms were reworked, and ceilings were raised wherever possible. Bullard decided to create a glamorous space with as much shine and reflection as possible, covering the ceilings in platinum leaf, adding baseboards of stainless steel, and even lining the powder room walls in a wallpaper made from Murano glass beads. A mirrored coffee table adds sparkle to a sitting area, while a long reflecting polished-metal

OPPOSITE: **A corner of the L-shaped living space has views of Century City and the distant beaches of Venice and Santa Monica. Here, zebra skin cushions add a graphic touch to the white B&B Italia sofas. The mirrored coffee table adds glassy reflections to the room.**

cabinet by 1970s furniture designer and sculptor Paul Evans faces the master bed. Furnish and Bullard discovered a chandelier that used to hang over the front desk in Milan's Grand Hotel, which adds just the right amount of shimmering drama to the open kitchen.

Texture was important, too: Bullard brought in expansive soft-white goatskin rugs for the floor and added a python-upholstered bed to the richly dark main bedroom suite, as well as pieces of his own design when necessary, such as the living room's onyx and chrome coffee tables that glow from within.

The art that Furnish and Bullard chose provided the considerable impact of bold contemporary work; hanging on bright green walls in the sitting room is a huge painting by Chinese artist Wang Guangyi, and smaller pieces by Damien Hirst and Dale Chihuly add shine and reflections to the mirrored coffee table.

OPPOSITE: The bright green living room walls extend into the kitchen. The chandelier once hung over the front desk of the Grand Hotel in Milan. The kitchen island is big enough to do double duty in this moderately sized space as a dining table, with its rows of purple and chrome Italian bar stools. ABOVE: Martyn Lawrence Bullard transformed the passageways into a galleries to showcase part of Elton John's extensive collection of the work of American photographer William Eggleston. FOLLOWING SPREAD: On a clear day, John's upper floor apartment has breathtaking views of Los Angeles. Set on a goatskin rug in the living room, chrome and onyx coffee tables, designed by the decorator, are lit from within. Here, small sculptures by Dale Chihuly and Damien Hirst add to the tabletop collection of art and books.

241

LEFT: The primary bed is upholstered in python skin; the walls have been plastered a restful Venetian brown. The neon work above the bed is by artist Tracey Emin; the painting is by Gary Hume.
ABOVE: A classic Pierre Paulin Ribbon red chair sits in front of a silver metal curtain.

SHIRE HOUSE
BY JOSEF VAN DER KAR
ECHO PARK

Artist Peter Shire lives with his wife, Donna, in the Echo Park house he grew up in. Next door to Silver Lake, back in 1910, this early Los Angeles neighborhood was the first center of filmmaking in the city. It also has the distinction of being the location of the first pie-in-the-face movie scene.

Like Silver Lake, Echo Park is named for its lake, which was originally a reservoir. Since the 1950s, the population has been heavily Latino, so Shire has grown up with the colorful buildings that continue to inspire his work today. Now, it is also a hip neighborhood with plenty of nightlife.

Peter's father, Henry Shire, was a craftsman and builder, and he commissioned Josef Van der Kar, a mid-century modern architect, to design a house that he proceeded to build himself. This single-story 1,400-square-foot

**FURNISHINGS
BY PETER SHIRE**

house now has a landmark designation, and his son has been careful not to alter its original footprint. An open-plan living-dining area is filled with natural light by large floor-to-ceiling windows, which lead out to a terrace and garden designed by legendary garden designer Garrett Eckbo.

The only American who took part in Memphis, the famous Italian designer group that defined the 1980s, Shire has always taken a prominent role in shaping design in Los Angeles with his public sculptures and murals. He has built his life and work in this neighborhood, and has a large studio nearby filled with his own pottery, furniture, art, and sculpture.

Bright colors begin the approach to the house, where Shire has even matched his red car to the front door, while the shingled redwood exterior is enlivened by turquoise window trim. Indoors, the fireplace is anchored by

OPPOSITE: The terra-cotta tiling runs throughout the Shire House. Here, red chairs, by Shire, are from 2007. The house was granted Historic-Cultural Monument status by the City of Los Angeles. FOLLOWING SPREAD: The combined living and dining room includes Gio Ponti Superleggera chairs around a dining table made by Shire's father. A photograph of Shire's parents' first meeting hangs above. Shire designed the TV cabinet, which was inspired by the set for a Punch and Judy show he had seen on a TV program.

a brick wall, while the rest of the walls are the original panels of birch plywood. In the dining room, Shire displays one of his signature armchairs in bold, colorful, abstract shapes. He resourcefully recovered his mother's sofa in pale green velvet trimmed with unexpectedly bold passementerie. The center of attention is the television, tented with red-striped fabric, inspired by the British Punch and Judy puppet shows. The colorful bookcase is filled with Shire's ceramics and a collection of vintage *kokeshi* dolls, a nod to Donna's Japanese heritage.

A large vintage photo of Shire's parents overlooks the dining area, which includes a table made by Henry, Gio Ponti Superleggera chairs, and a pair by Charles Eames, once owned by his father but reworked by Shire junior. The largest bedroom was designed with a folding screen to split it into

childhood bedrooms for Peter and his brother, Billy. It has views out to the back garden, full of avocado and lemon trees.

Since Shire's formative Memphis years, he has been highly productive, producing ceramics—teapots, mugs, and other works in clay—as well as a never-ending stream of innovative chairs, tables, and sofas. Furnishing his own house has never been a challenge for him—today it has become a comfortable merger between two generations of artists.

OPPOSITE: The living space has a large bookcase filled with Shire's ceramics, glassware, teapots, and sculpture. A couch from Shire's mother was reupholstered with olive green velvet and outsize welting and tassels. ABOVE, LEFT: Shire's silver-plated 1982 Anchorage teapot was made for Memphis. The Shire portrait is by his late father. ABOVE, RIGHT: More art pieces are on display, including several by Shire's father.

PAGE 252: Shire has repainted the original kitchen cabinets pink and yellow. PAGE 253: The exterior patio in the garden, originally laid out by Garrett Eckbo, has new framing. RIGHT: The main bedroom looks directly out to the garden, which is filled with avocado and lemon trees.

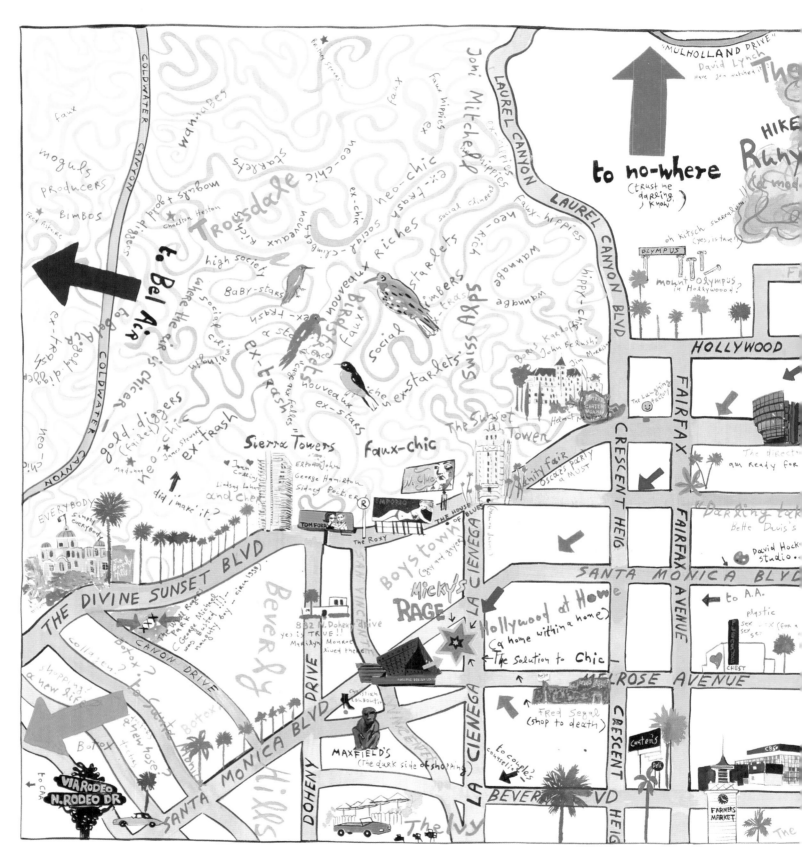

"Star Map" by Konstantin Kakanias exclusively for Hollywood at Home by Peter Dunham